Irina Ragl

Identification

I move into the spirit of the perfect model
I create and make it visible in its brightest colors!

Irina Ragl
Identification

I move into the spirit of the perfect model I create and make it visible in its brightest colors!

Translated from the German by Irina Ragl
Editing: Penelope Vernet
Assistance: Martin Ragl

Original Title: Identifikation.
Copyright © 2011 Irina Ragl
Production and Publishing: Books on Demand GmbH, Norderstedt

ISBN: 978-3-8423-3553-0

Email: Leben-in-Balance@gmx.at

Irina Ragl

Identification

I move into the spirit of the perfect model
I create and make it visible in its brightest colors!

A creativity book

My friends, I know nothing less flexible
than the mind without practice.

My friends, I know nothing more supple
than the mind with practice.

My friends, I know nothing that creates such crime
as the mind without practice.

My friends, I know nothing that creates such blessings
as the mind with practice.

My friends, I know nothing that leads to such outrage
as the mind without practice.

My friends, I know nothing that leads to such supreme happiness
as the mind with practice.

G.B.

Preface

Dear reader,

Real thoughts are true thoughts.
Real thoughts come from a higher level.
Real thoughts come through a pure mind.
Real thoughts are in harmony with the LAW.
Real thoughts are endowed with love,
wisdom and power, able to enlighten,
to heal and to help us prosper.
Real thoughts are creative.
Real thoughts bring real joyfulness and the best results for all.
Real thoughts are eternal and always new.
Real thoughts set us free.

Surface thoughts are reactions and reflections.
Surface thoughts are here
at the moment and forgotten tomorrow.
Surface thoughts create chaos and keep us in bondage.

The difference between surface thoughts
and real thoughts is like the difference between
noise and music.
If you want to be free, you have to think truth.
If you want to think truth, you had best avoid noise.

Leave the outside appearances aside
and think your inner truth into reality!

Your holy heart is the pivotal point
between your mind and practice.

Life is a blessing as soon as you discover,
accept and honor how wonderful you are.

The moment you are aware of your greatness,
you are able to perceive the greatness in all.

How high do you want to go?
If you like, use this book as a launching
pad for your own dreams:

Be creative!

Develop mental and emotional strength!

Think elevated thoughts and *identify* with them!

Making the best of yourself and experiencing your eternal,
marvellous truths is the greatest pleasure.

52 lessons to accompany you on your path
from mental to miracle-working, intuitive consciousness

Thank God and all of humanity!
May every new day unfold even more harmoniously and happily
than the day before!

My name is:

....

I AM

I am!

Oh yes, I am!
Therefore I can understand these words.

I am what I make out of myself through my thinking.

I am as small as I let falsehood and fear restrict me – or as great as I believe in and cherish myself.

Greatness is neither a question of age, possession, external power nor prestige.

The more I dwell in myself, and evolve and give from my true source, the greater I become.

My drawings and mind-maps

e.g.: Do I use people, objects or activities to define myself?

Do I have a profound self-image?

How do I improve the way I feel about myself each day?

The best is yet to be revealed.

I live to prosper, to make progress, to live more and in a better way.
Continually being more and manifesting more is the path to wealth, health
and happiness!

To accept my greatness within my heart gives me the motivation and
strength to do better.
Expanding my awareness and improving myself allow my hidden powers,
abilities and talents to come forth.

I am able to be healthy, happy and prosperous whenever I endeavour
to make my unique self visible, to share what I have, to make my own
dreams come true.

By bringing my inner wealth into the outer, I increase my gladness and my
joy of life.
In doing so, I am not taking anything away from anyone: with me, the
whole world becomes richer and more beautiful!

My drawings and mind-maps

e.g.: Why am I doing the things I do?
Do I feel grateful when I fall asleep at night?
Do I wake up inspired and full of anticipated joy
about the day to come?

My delight at achieving and my success begin with honest answers to the
questions:

WHAT DO I REALLY VALUE?

and

WHO DO I BELIEVE I CAN BE?

Being thankful, sound and great motivates me to do grand things, and I am
the one to decide and accept how good I am.
A clear vision of myself and what I love to do and create is the basic
requirement for a constructive way of life.
What good are other people´s pictures, however wonderful, if I do not
have my own?
As I design a clear idea of a happy future in my mind, my will can unfold
its power.

My imagination is working ceaselessly in all areas of my life.
I move in the exact direction of my conscious and subconscious pictures.

Until I make myself aware of my unconscious programming and beliefs
and the possibility of changing them, they will dominate my life and I will
call it destiny.

Making myself aware of the mental and spiritual faculties the Creator
has put at my disposal and using them in the proper way will lead me to
freedom and mastery.

My drawings and mind-maps

e.g.: I become what I treasure:
Reclaiming full responsibility gives me the freedom to decide:
I choose my identity:
My mental and spiritual faculties:

My soul is a heart in the superconscious.

I cultivate my precise vision:

I acknowledge my inner reality,
I pay attention for what is in harmony with my innermost self,
I imagine exactly what I will manifest,
I expect it and welcome it with a grateful heart.

My sunny, well-defined image and my presence of mind keep me
unsusceptible.
Outside influences can only affect me if I allow my feelings to hold on to
them.

As soon as I fully identify with my dream, I achieve my goals in a playful
and harmonious way.

My drawings and mind-maps

e.g.: "Let there be light!"
(Light is the excelsior idea, the divine consciousness):
Pure heart, clear vision:
I get what I ask for:
I am dedicated, I am able:

How can I transform old, wrong, negative, partially unconscious pictures into positive ones?

I am becoming aware:

First:
All blockages, anger, fears, doubts, sorrow have been caused by my upbringing or by illusion and are not a part of my true self.

Second:
I am not here to pay for my karma, I am here to learn the laws of life!

Third:
All problems can be dissolved by charity, concentration and accurate knowledge.
Higher knowledge is power – the strength and power to forgive!

My drawings and mind-maps

e.g.: I express my feelings freely and spontaneously:
My negative and my positive emotions:
My negative emotions help me identify my wrong beliefs:
What do I want to change or improve?

I do not oppose what is negative.
It will be transformed into something good the moment I have changed my conception:

By holding a true image I maintain my peace of mind in the midst of chaotic thoughts.
My faith and thankfulness make me immune.

With loving kindness, understanding and goodwill, it is easier to contribute to a solution.

Calmly I can face all distractions without reacting to them. I am feeling steadfast, complete and confident.

As soon as I understand the lesson to be learned and I base my thinking on true knowledge, difficulties instantly disappear!

With determination and enthusiasm I continue my path.

Optimism, humor and gratitude keep me strong and healthy and are also the most effective cosmetic agents.

Thanks to my enlightened thoughts and feelings, healing forces can do their work.
It is always a convincing, positive intention that activates healing forces through my sub-conscious mind.

My drawings and mind-maps

e.g.: Non-resistance gives me the possibility to observe:
I take time to learn:
Ways that help me to control my mood, to raise my vibration:

I cannot force my imagination. I cannot dictate my convictions.
I need insight and practice!

Decidedly, with patience and perseverance I sow into my subconscious
the seeds of new, real thoughts and images.
This diminishes inner conflicts and disputes and helps me keep a
harmonious state of mind.

The inner force is benevolent and acts in an orderly way!
Whenever I perceive this power in my soul, it brings peace to my mind
and serenity to my feelings.

I become receptive to my higher consciousness. My intuition grows
stronger and inspires my creative imagination.

I focus on what is good and make it better.

My drawings and mind-maps

e.g.: Who gets my attention? What do I agree with?
I remember the gentleness of my heart:
I eliminate unproductive emotions by watchfulness,
releasing and fulfilling actions,
based on love and respect:

My self-awareness brings me self-confidence.
Each positive thought is a perception of truth.
A positive thought about myself is an understanding of my true self.

My current appearance, my charm, my health, my resilience,
my ability to perform, my friendships, my social contacts,
my creativity, my authenticity, my capacities,
my ability to experience joy, my adaptability, my wealth,
all these are reflections of my insights about my inner being,
of how I use my spiritual forces and the universal laws of life.

Real success is the fruit of a true thought to which I commit myself and for
which I assume responsibility.

A conviction inspired by the awareness of truth creates good feelings and
a positive vibration, which determine my actions and are the cause of my
achievements and my good results.

My drawings and mind-maps

e.g.: How much time do I take for those things
that make my life more significant and precious?
What I hold in my mind determines my reality:
I identify with my own original thoughts:

My clear understanding and the constructive use of my inner
persuasiveness enable me to reach ever higher goals.

Love, faith and awareness are the food of my soul.
My own higher understanding liberates me.

Becoming aware of the process of thinking is the key issue in any genuine
philosophy and religion.

I attain freedom through self-discipline, by learning to use my spiritual
faculties and to think in a self-determined manner.
To the decree that I choose my thoughts, that I check my feelings and
correct myself, I am able to design my own life the way I actually like it.

My drawings and mind-maps

e.g.: I have options, I have hope:
True thoughts – pure feelings – real food:
Gratitude connects me with the source of supply:
I put my mind to work:

The miracle-working power of persuasion operates within me!
There is no work more rewarding than becoming aware of that force
in action and cooperating harmoniously with all conscious and
subconscious spiritual powers in the achievement of my self-determined
goal, in materializing my own dream.

I hold my well-defined image with enthusiasm:
I visualize it and appreciate it until it comes true.

The original work takes place inside me, and through my courageous,
intelligent actions my insights turn into abilities.

To work means to love, to increase life.
I replace all "hard work" with empathy, wisdom and inspired actions.
To work is to believe in my eternal, infinite, inner wealth, to express it and
share it beneficially.

My drawings and mind-maps

e.g.: My favorite project, which I resolve to complete by ...
Heartfelt work instead of hard work:
What am I prepared to become,
to (for-)give and to do in order to experience
my dream?

Everything begins with respecting all of me, listening to my gut feelings, being faithful to my inner truth and recognizing the perfect being that I am.

Accepting my higher self means serving the law of life!

Tension and pressure are the result of foreign rules, of being alienated from myself.
Honesty and hope bring me back into harmony with myself and lead to insight and freedom, so that I can succeed in understanding my inner forces and apply them creatively to develop my life.

By embracing my higher consciousness I can ally myself with my current situation and make it bear fruit.
This is the way to make sense of my life, to reveal the meaning of my life.

My drawings and mind-maps

e.g.: I am not driven, I thrive:
I surrender to fairness:
I focus on the real me:
I dare to write out my ideal:
I live from inside out:

My ideas and pictures, my questions and answers

My genius lies within, waiting to be recognized.

The purpose of all education is to gain clarity about my soul-values and to learn the proper use of all my creative faculties, so that I can express them continually and consciously.

The desires of my heart show me the way.
Boldly I invest my energy in uplifting activities which address my unconscious, limiting beliefs and help me to heal them. Challenging goals are goals that advance me.

Others will give me as much credit as I have the courage to trust in myself and to believe in a fabulous future.
I am valued by others to the degree that I am aware of my own worth.

Experience confirms my self-awareness and my self-confidence.

My drawings and mind-maps

e.g.: I deserve - I am good enough:
My self-worth - My self-image:
I count - I am precious:
My material income - My psychic income:

Every moment I begin a new life with a higher awareness, making
something new, something better come true.

I obey and trust the infinite, miracle-working power and the law within.
God´s loving presence flows in and through me like a golden stream and
lets me live to see the world from a healed point of view!
My inner being, the spirit in me, is always safe, supported and curious.

This positive attitude turns each day into a source of gratitude!

In difficulties I look for opportunities.
I preserve my calmness of mind and fill my consciousness with kindness,
wisdom and strength.

My drawings and mind-maps

e.g.: I dress for success:
I rejoice in the blessings I can give and receive today:
I believe in my well-being, in my prosperity and love them into results:
My actions are based on understanding and faith:

Self-determination requires self-reliance, autonomy and self-discipline.
Those only flourish if I help myself:

I make my own decisions. I give myself clear instructions and I stick to
them.

I stay focused on my goal with optimism in my soul and fully rely on the
inner power that assists me.
This gives me the opportunity to unfold my whole being – body, soul and
spirit – in a balanced way.

My thoughts, feelings and actions are in accordance with my goal.
With affirmations I confirm that my dream is true, despite any indications
to the contrary! Thanks to my affirmations, my consciousness and my
subconscious keeps co-creating in a positive way and so fulfil my wishes.
This is wonderful!

My drawings and mind-maps

e.g.: I choose intuitively illumined growth rather than being changed:
Through single-heartedness and simplicity in all areas of my life,
I improve my ability to visualize and focus with ease:
My favourite truth-statements and guiding principles
that keep me on course:

I behold the good in everything!

I say yes to myself.
I say yes to my life.
I say yes to my growth.
I say yes to my goal.
I say yes to my empowerment.
I say yes to my health, my happiness and my success.
I say yes to my environment and the people around me.
I say yes to the well-being of us all.

More and more doors open up for me to express my creativity:

All that is good is waiting to be recognized!
As I appreciate and accept the best the universe is always willing to give
me, I do not have to be satisfied with second best.

I expect the very best in any situation!

My drawings and mind-maps

e.g.: In love with my clear vision, I trustfully give it freedom to evolve: "I let go and let God" – I let go of controlling the outcome by moving in the right direction consistently and with joy:

I bless and release negative and compulsive ideas and circumstances,
disempowering them by holding my attention confidently and diligently
on a higher order.
My courageous decision to give my best provides me instant relief.

My thankful and cheerful attitude towards life and my noble-mindedness
keep me in harmony with the laws of life.
I am surrounded by a world of harmony, peace and joy as soon as my
thoughts, feelings and actions are tuned to the frequency of mutual
respect, understanding and support.

God´s love fulfils us.
Divine wisdom constantly manifests through us.

To follow the law of life is to love.
From this arises a determination of heart that attracts all means, all help,
all forces, all marvellous opportunities.

My drawings and mind-maps

e.g.: I transcend my family patterns:
How do I handle other peoples opinions and behavior?
I stay aware of what is most important at any moment:
How can I create space for a higher level of self-love for all?

Winning is the reward for not quitting, even if I fail, but for serenely maintaining my focus on my goal until it is achieved.

I do not meditate over the part of myself that lives in duality, in that illusory world of oppositions.
I am whole, embedded in the greater whole. In this awareness of wholeness my forces and possibilities are unlimited!

My creative imagination opens up to me a truly joyful, harmonious world of abundance, the causal world, the inner kingdom.
This is where the meaning is hidden – universal and eternal, immutable and ever new.

My drawings and mind-maps

e.g.: I let my gains and failures teach me new ways of usefulness and
expand the variety of possibilities for growth:
I stay focused on the main thing:
The purpose of my life:

Thanks to my gift for visualizing and my determination, I can express as much of my inner greatness as I wish.

My faith in a higher reality leads me and fires my imagination.
Everything is possible, as soon as I understand that it is possible.

I free myself from all limiting points of view and accept inner help and guidance in realizing my ideals.
My exhilarating and wise thoughts neutralize all doubts.

Because I know about a brilliant life and because I am ready to have it, I am able to make it visible by directing my imagination in the appropriate way.

It is on the power of self-persuasion that my results in life depend.

My drawings and mind-maps

e.g.: Life meant me to be fully alive, healthy and fortunate:
What do I commit myself to?
This is how I can implement my new ideas:
I build momentum playing life on the highest level possible:

The past is over. While my lack of knowledge and my ignorance of the spiritual laws could once cause me harm and hinder my development, I am now able through better understanding to fully forgive myself.

I look forward and I look upwards.
The present moment is the starting point of a continually happier and more fulfilled life.
I create my future more pleasant in every way.

Only what inspires me and uplifts me shall accompany me on my path.
My memory is a treasury of enlightening and precious pictures.
Storing good memories creates a perfect memory!

By deliberately turning my attention to what is worthwhile, I withdraw all power from what is negative and consciously connect to the Spirit within me, who helps me see through all illusions.

My drawings and mind-maps

e.g.: The one I can forgive the least I have to forgive the most:
I watch the starry sky:
The incomparable morning breeze brings me purity and clarity:
I experience the sunrise:

My honest readiness to forgive and to be forgiven makes clear decisions easy.

Thanks to my worthy ideal, all decisions serve to advance me. My higher consciousness keeps correcting them for something even better.

I repeatedly set my attention on which world I decide to live in.

While progressively realizing my vision, I constantly activate all positive powers that are stored in my heart: freedom, peace, health, love, friendship, gratitude, harmony, mindfulness and the boundless means to express and unfold my unique self.

I consciously nourish and strengthen true thoughts.
From now on I only speak about things that I desire and invite!

I quietly live in the present, with the certitude that I can cope with all tasks.
Everything I do with courage and joy increases my strength and success.

My drawings and mind-maps

e.g.: I do not live what I see on the news, in the media,
what is fashionable;
I live my dream!
I am responsible for my interpretation of the world!
Purposeful resolutions empower me and keep my way clear:

Being magnanimous and poised requires psychic, moral, spiritual and
physical development.

Constructive thinking means constructive feeling and constructive acting.
An active, practical and dynamic life makes my enterprises profitable.

I do not run after happiness, I am walking along with it!
From today onwards I am an achiever.
My subconscious gives me full support.

My positive subconscious connects me to the source of life and provides
me with the ability to be fully accountable for my life, my thoughts, my
feelings and actions.

Supply and security come from within. I am aware of it.
A winning aura of self-assurance surrounds me.
I express it through my centered behavior.

My drawings and mind-maps

e.g.: My attitude towards life determines the world I live in:
My positive subconscious:
As I stay consciously connected,
I am provided with what I really want and what serves me the best:

As soon as I can feel I will be well, that my wishes will be fulfilled, I stop
forcing good luck, which always leads to the opposite of what I desire.
If willpower and imagination come into conflict, it is imagination that
wins.

Whenever my willpower and my imagination work together, my attention
stays focused on the realisation of my goal.

By thankfully and confidently handing all my wishes over to my helpful
superconscious, I experience a powerful breakthrough in my creative
powers.
Without calculation, everything turns out so much better than anything my
intellect ever could have taken in consideration.

Spontaneous surprises and higher impulses always bring something
wonderful to my life!

My drawings and mind-maps

e.g.: What do I allow myself to have and to be right now?
I am happy, because I make it happen:
I am flexible and open-minded:
Thanks to my inner stability, I dare to keep discovering new,
unknown spheres of life:

The certainty that with the right mindset everything good comes to me
naturally and by law makes me humble, helpful and generous.

Due to my loving thoughts for all, my subconscious mind brings forth
everything that is miraculous and supportive, all mirthfulness, all health
and all success.
II rejoice in assisting others in achieving goals that cause them to grow
and feel more dignified.
Immeasurable abundance surrounds us!

My love lets me see the yet invisible perfection within each of us and in
any situation.
It gives my will the right direction.

I bless everything with an image of perfection!
My gratitude strengthens my faith and makes my actions productive and
harmonious.

Calmness of mind and patience are the highest speed.
On a higher level of consciousness, I have more time and space at my
disposal.
As I move toward my highest ideal with concentration, I have all the time
of eternity and can experience how all things continually transform into
something better.

My drawings and mind-maps

e.g.: I am at peace with the rhythmic process of life:
Agape makes me forbearing:
I am in control, awake and aware, capable of recognizing opportunities:
I like taking risks that correspond to my dream:

Lasting vitality accrues from being true to my vision.

My will finds the straight way to realization, as I support it with life-affirming thoughts and hopeful, grateful feelings.

My spirit fills time and space with glorious and optimistic mental images.
In approaching my goal I am carried on wings of gladness, conscious that
I am a winner at all times.
I dream my life and I live my dream.

Heart-guided visionaries are the most practical people. They create
a crystal clear image of their future and have the ability to make the
impossible possible.

With enthusiasm, discipline of thought and self-correction, I give my life
the direction I choose.

With my love, willpower and persistence, my vision turns into my outer
experience.

My drawings and mind-maps

e.g.: How can I raise my vitality?
I develop the awareness of heaven on earth:
I remember who I AM:
I take my ideas seriously:

Whenever my will to be me, to be free and to reach my goal is expressed through goal-oriented actions, my character refines and my credibility and enjoyment of life grow.

My desire and my will to be active and to create arise from my insight that all capabilities dwell within me.

My self-esteem becomes genuine and strong!
An atmosphere of confidence that wipes away all obstacles accompanies me.

My sense of humor enables me to see all things from different perspectives.

Profitable results follow on my originality and my determination.
I am the creative ruler of my mental and spiritual forces.

My drawings and mind-maps

e.g.: Success leads to more success:
I am resourceful and rejoice at every little triumph:
I keep the fire burning:

An ideal life requires that I have an ideal attitude towards life:
I cease fighting the useless fight against evil forever!

Self-liberation succeeds if I place trust solely in the one power within me
as well as in others and in all domains of life.

I have success as soon as I recognize that everything serves my good.
This also frees me from criticism and from the urge to judge.
I become truly wise.

I am at home within myself and listen only to the silent voice of my
intuition. I consciously stay in touch with the All-Good.

My drawings and mind-maps

e.g.: I let God embrace all that is:
I hold conscious contact, I stay in touch:
I perceive the amazing, wise guidance in my life:
I am receptive:

I am positive, strong and radiant by increasing my awareness of myself as one with the all-knowing, creating power.

I give from my inner abundance, which is ever accessible and unlimited. Everything meaningful in my life comes from this source.

The secret is that I create in inner wholeness and in harmony with the spiritual laws. I am constructing in silence. Co-creation begins when I am in silent unity with the infinite and in harmony with the universe. Creations that are based on the principles of life are a true blessing. They last and make sense.

By understanding, accepting and applying the universal laws I become an architect of heaven on earth.
I am thankful and evolve new faculties in order to accomplish the ever more perfect, and to improve life.

My drawings and mind-maps

e.g.: Which spiritual laws am I aware of?
I study them daily and use them deliberately and
more consciously all the time:
I get inspired by nature:

My faith is growing, because I trust the inner support-system.

I renounce demanding help, praise and approval from the outside.
I have the courage and boldness to expect everything from God!

Wherever I am, I let people experience how powerful they are when they
re-establish their faith in themselves:
Thought is the ruler of our life-force.
All thoughts focused on joy, forgiveness, justice, abundance, soundness
and prosperity, freedom, creativity and enlightenment disencumber our
souls and release new energy.
Our souls become healed and free, which leads to physical health,
happiness, fulfilment and fuller expression.

My drawings and mind-maps

e.g.: Life is always PRO! I believe this:
My wealth-consciousness:
Riches serve me the more I share them:

I acknowledge the interaction between body, soul and spirit and pay attention to a physiological balance.
I can solve blockages through relaxation, joy-filled movement and recognition of truth.

I immediately forget anything unpleasant. As soon as I dismiss it from my mind, it no longer affects me and I can re-establish my inner peace.

I let go and relax wherever I am.
I focus on the truth that sets me free, on the order I wish to realize in my life.

Joyful, effortless movements lift me out of the heaviness of the body and strengthen all the forces related to my body, mind and soul.

By setting truths into motion I keep returning to the flow of life!

My inner equilibrium is reflected in natural, caring and balanced relationships with the people around me and with society.
My sunny mentality and my positive radiance make me a strong personality.

My drawings and mind-maps

e.g.: … singing, dancing, hiking, sailing, gardening …
I bring new and playful elements into my life:
My inner and my outer posture:
My coherence enables me
to fully appreciate the present moment:

My no means no and my yes means yes!
I understand the power and might of creative thinking.
The order in my thoughts and feelings brings order into my world.

How I experience life is my awareness translated into reality!

The sensation of life that I am looking for is created by the clarity and
purity of my conscious and unconscious mind-powers.
The harmony between my conscious and my unconscious mind
determines to what extent my thoughts are in accord with my feelings and
activities.

I clean my subconscious of all negative paradigms.
This enables my conscious mind, subconscious mind and superconscious
mind to work together in unity:
My all-wise, eternal being comes forth. The world of miracles becomes
reality!

My intuitive thinking and feeling are not restricted by exterior
appearances.
They cause me to be aware of my own eternal truths and to express them.

My drawings and mind-maps

e.g.: What is the difference between mental and intuitive consciousness?
How can I raise my awareness:
I embody a higher dimension of me:

In all situations I set my activities toward my sublime vision.
Positive pictures, supported by my faith, bring about a radiating power and persistence, which even build through obstacles and make me do the right thing at all times.

Thanks to thoughts and feelings, illumined by holistic contents, I become able to experience an orderly universe, and to understand and apply the laws of ever-expanding life.

My loyalty to my worthy ideal helps me overcome all negative states of mind.
In this way I overcome the world; I belong neither to the oppressed nor the oppressors.
I am free to live the life I create in my dreams, which leads me higher and higher.

My drawings and mind-maps

e.g.: Gratitude – Faith – Determination:
I respect healthy boundaries
and don´t make other people´s problems my problems:
I create a fantastic environment that nourishes my positive expectations:
Amazing synchronicities:

My yes-I-can attitude turns every challenge into an adventure.
The adventure lies in maintaining the unity within myself.

In this unity the law of attraction can work!
My wishes come true all by themselves.

The certitude that God knows better "how" and that the all-present cosmic consciousness takes care of everything in my life fills me with serenity and praise.

I am enthusiastic about life!
My gratitude for who I am and what I have brings me what I am working toward more quickly.

My drawings and mind-maps

e.g.: When does the law of attraction work?
How do miracles become natural and daily experiences in my life?
All good that´s there is also there for me!
I give my best and I have it all!

True faith is integrity, a positive attitude, the recognition of the inner order, trust in the law of attraction.

In harmony with the universe I experience the omnipresent grace of God. God´s all-encompassing love also loves me, lives and works through me! My mind fulfils its function when it makes me more aware of this.

The responsibility for my life resides in my choice of thoughts. True, cheerful thoughts enable me to think clearly, to activate dormant faculties, to discover possibilities, to develop creative ideas, to plan methodically, to act wisely and to take control of my own life.

My new point of view reveals a new perception to me: experiencing God´s omnipresence … is my intuitive, miracle-working consciousness!

My drawings and mind-maps

e.g.: I balance my feminine and my masculine energies:
I manage my freedom through eternal love and integrity:
Whenever I have reached my goal,
I enhance the good in life and set a new and higher one:
Divine love enlivens my faith:

No other person, no organization, no government can manifest my good.
My constant, conscious unity with the infinite results in the appearance of
abundance.

I use the powers I have been given to design my life with love and
intelligence.

The law of attraction serves my very own evolution.
Aiming high opens up new spheres of life.

I follow my intuition and experience that I am a spiritual being, a divine
being, meant to be free and wealthy.

My drawings and mind-maps

e.g.: With how many riches am I in harmony?
I do what only I can do:
I give myself permission to be who I want to be,
to do what I want to do and
to have what I want to have:

My heart gives all attention to the oneness of the conscious mind,
subconscious mind and superconscious mind.
"Men must not divide what God has united!"

This wholeness is the basis for my sincere attitude and for my inner
balance!

The silent voice inside tells me about my true destiny: with my thoughts I
can design my life as I wish!

When my thoughts, feelings and actions correspond with my intuition, my
life has a harmonious, enriching effect on all.

My drawings and mind-maps

e.g.: I look at everything with wholeness in mind:
Praxis is the mother of learning:
Light creates through me:

My decision to be supported and instructed from within fills me with a sense of security.
To consciously connect my breath with spirit makes my heart smile!

My heart reveals to me the purpose of my life, the perfect plan, together with all the means and ways to realize it.
I trust in the omnipresent principle of divine love, which does everything for me: it loves me reliably, heals, supplies, nourishes, protects, illumines and inspires me.

When I listen to my inner guidance, I go upwards.

I am learning better and better how to follow my intuition.
I make use of the desires of my very own heart.
Wonderful things happen in my life because I act on higher inspirations.

I enshrine a place of silence inside me and give all confidence to this wise and loving power.
My inner knowing always leads me to the right place and to what is good for me.

My drawings and mind-maps

e.g.: I obey my inner voice, not the outer noise:
In peace and quiet I capture the essence:
Out of the silence I gain my might and authority:

Courageously I demand my good.
Thankfully I accept the joy, the benevolence and the generosity of life.
Every day I expand my acceptance for the better.

I claim my freedom to continually multiply the good in and around me!
Self-development and ever more perfect self-expression are essentials in
human life.
The infinite is inexhaustible.
The good I am looking for is also looking for me.

On a higher level of awareness, everything serves my good, cleanses and
refines my thoughts and aspirations and helps me unfold new faculties.
I submit neither to doubts, nor fears, nor forebodings;
the superconsciousness knows only one power: the universal good.

My drawings and mind-maps

e.g.: I mind my own business:
I dare, I do and I am silent:
I share, I show up and I speak up:

My thankful calmness intensifies the dynamics of positive progress. Safety and authentic luxury nurture my creativity, my ability to serve and my productive power.

I practice my oneness with the divine consciousness!

Every clear, true thought lightens my mind and strengthens my conviction that my higher consciousness has an answer to all my questions. It finds a solution for problems where there seems to be none and is ready to grant my intentions.

My love and gratitude bring me in harmony with a higher perception and make me discover that I am IN-DIVISIBLY united with omnipresent love, wisdom, power and substance:

I experience my IN-DIVID-UALITY!

My drawings and mind-maps

e.g.: My life on the creative plane, in collaboration with the infinite:
I can ask for help and graciously accept it:
I become an innovator who can solve problems
before they even show up:

I perform with dignity from my inner realisation:
Wherever I go, I feel a warm welcome from within myself.

I have a natural aplomb.
I do what I love to do.
With vigor and zest I fulfil my self-chosen duties.

The greater my love and my vision, the greater my persistence and my self-conquest.

Pure love and conscious awareness preserve my sovereignty.

My drawings and mind-maps

e.g.: Happiness and optimism is what I want to cultivate:
My professional performance:
I think in energies:

Gratitude is true happiness.
My honest approval of myself and my life induce me to impart in an enlightening and loving manner.

Using all my faculties wisely, I can serve life better and better and thereby increase my well-being.

I prosper the more I give.

To give from the infinite is the only life-sustaining principle!

Wherever I am, of my own free will I give from the divine abundance.

My drawings and mind-maps

e.g.: How can I delight others today?
By knowing my unique talents I can serve life best:
Coaches, mentors, friends that inspire me to contribute my gifts
and help me stay on track:

I live in the world I imagine.
I see my own consciousness.

I get what I give.
I get what I think, feel, say and do.
I get what I am.

I am love!
Love connects and makes me attract true bliss.

I comply with the law of love by my pleasure in giving!

Giving what I create through my conscious oneness with the source of abundance makes the dream of love a reality!

My drawings and mind-maps

e.g.: Like attracts like. My vibration is decisive:
I root myself in love and truth:
I connect, interact and collaborate with joy, ease and integrity!

I give my best to the world and the best comes to me.

I not only forgive all that is unworthy and destructive, I forget it.
I establish my picture of a worthy ideal and hold it with love, faith and
goodwill.

Unconditional love is true giving.
I follow my heart and give away pure love.

I give joyfully from abundance, and abundance increases.

My drawings and mind-maps

e.g.: A new life asks for new, merry pictures:
I can bring new values into this world:
The bright colors of grace:

To give what I receive from the Supreme brings harmony.

True giving makes me aware of my unlimited inner riches and lets them circulate.
True giving makes me calm and jubilant.
True giving makes me recognize, adore and praise the Creator, who is immeasurably powerful, supportive and inventive.

True giving solves every conflict.
True giving opens up a higher consciousness.
True giving inspires and keeps me experiencing my unity with the infinite.

I am one with the Divine Spirit, and I acknowledge it in everyone.

My drawings and mind-maps

e.g.: I come from a higher place:
I honor and respect myself and others no matter what:
To really know something I have to love it first:

I get what I give and give what I am.

I am consciousness!
What I am conscious of – in other words, what I think and believe about
myself, about my fellow humans and the world – is what I continually
give to my subconscious ... And this is what I get in return.

I appreciate and understand the world I am living in.
I love and understand myself and know where I am going.

Forgiveness, goodwill and grateful giving purify my life, my thoughts and
my feelings.
I am what I want to be at this very moment!
I have the power!

Such giving is true living and manifests as grateful happiness in the
smallest things.

My drawings and mind-maps

e.g.: I identify with the very thing I like to bring into my life:
I am willing to be free, creating the life I envision:
Living my dream, I start each day by being absolutely honest,
doing first what is most important:

I give at first, making it a habit to pay attention to my inspirations and to realize my ideas immediately, acting in a way that does justice to my highest conceptions.

I trust the Almighty and give thanks in advance with pleasant anticipation.

I go the "extra mile", always ready to discover new possibilities and grand qualities in myself and in others.

My alert interest makes life interesting.
In order to live my dream, it is important to wake up, to awaken my spirit and my soul.
Being awake, being interested, being aware, having presence of mind are fundamental to my progression.

My drawings and mind-maps

e.g.: My new, beneficial, profitable habits:
It is fun to learn:
This is the way I sculpt my day:

Love is the order and harmony of ever-expanding life!

What lives, and therefore constantly renews and improves, is eternal.

My genuine, constructive interest increases my understanding.
Through my understanding, my faith and my love grow.

Everything I love advances me.

I see how well I understand other people.
My success in business, my friendships, my marriage, my happiness in life thrive in my ability to communicate.

My drawings and mind-maps

e.g.: The better I understand myself, the better I understand others:
In a good temper it is easy to communicate:
I refine the art of listening:

To grow means to love more, understand more and share more.

I always look for new possibilities to assist others in their growth.

With a higher awareness we can improve everything: our health, our qualities, our faculties and talents, our relationships, our finances, our success and our happiness.

All things fall into place as soon as we recognize and experience our oneness with the source of life.

My consciousness is a present of life to me, full of promise: how I use it is my present to life.

My drawings and mind-maps

e.g.: What kind of recognition, commendation or reward do I integrate?
What kind of recognition, commendation and reward am I ready to give?
How do I participate in the group dynamics of the Spirit in my life?

Consciously I use my intellectual faculties to extend and improve every area of my life:

I know why!
My INTUITION tells me: "Be-cause!"
Because I am the master of my life when I belong to the cause and not to the effect.

My PERCEPTION allows me to consider everything from different points of view.
With tolerance, forgiveness and open-mindedness I can take higher vantage points and perceive new ways and possibilities.

With my REASON I decide what I want to be, to do and to have.
With certainty my reason chooses ideas that strengthen my faith in a higher reality.

With my IMAGINATION I design clear pictures. Nothing is too good to be true!

Purposively, poised and confident, my WILL focuses my attention on my goal.
I act full of hope, as if the desired were already realized.

My MEMORY knows the order in all things. I bear my source in mind and act from my center.

For that I am grateful.

My drawings and mind-maps

e.g.: For what purpose have I been given my intellectual faculties:
How do I apply them?
I become a master in who I am.

My consciousness clears up.
I see myself in a new light and learn to comprehend my greatness!

I look with the inner eyes of understanding, and my admiration for all life deepens.

Because I am prepared to give up old concepts - of myself, of others and the world - life reveals itself in ever expanding dimensions.

My drawings and mind-maps

e.g.: I make a difference by becoming different:
Every cell of my body tingles with praise and approval:
I make space for more good to come:
Beauty manifests through me:

When I live in harmony with all that surrounds me, life carries me!

I enjoy my freedom and let others be free to design their lives as their hearts desire.

My thoughts of harmony and confidence create an atmosphere of peace.

Peace is the highest form of wisdom!
Peace is wisdom made manifest.

Beauty surrounds me and makes the pleasure of peace evident to all.

My drawings and mind-maps

e.g.: I completely let go of what I want to prevent and allow
miracles to happen naturally:
With inner peace, the world appears in a gorgeous light:
I have everything for the mere thought of it:

My lively faith works!
I experience that I receive what I radiate.

I complete what I begin in preparation for the next step: a greater
awareness.

It is a privilege to consciously grow and to learn.
Daily the universe provides me with what I need.

As the water flows downwards to the sea and the fire leaps upwards
to its source, so do I move towards my true home: my ever expanding
awareness, my cosmic consciousness.

My drawings and mind-maps

e.g.: From chaos - to karma - to cosmos:
If love is complete everything can come true;
the impossible may just take a little longer:
I am in the flow of glowing colors:

I celebrate the miracle of my life.
I sing the song of my heart.

I am grounded and at home in myself.

I bring myself in.
I belong.

We celebrate the miracle of being alive!

My drawings and mind-maps

e.g.: Which feelings do the different celebrations call forth in me?
What do I celebrate and how?
The symphony of evolving:

Only those who know themselves can share.

Only those who have can give.

Only those who give can receive.

I know myself.

I love myself.

I design myself.

e.g.: With higher awareness, all things are possible:
I transform by making quantum leaps and get to keep
the awareness I gain from the process:
From now on I live a life of wonders and enthusiasm: